KEY STAGE 1

Year 1 | Term 2

Teaching and Learning

Science

Activity Book

Andrew Hodges

Alan Jarvis

Heather Monaghan

First published 2001

Letts Educational Ltd, The Chiswick Centre,
414 Chiswick High Road, London W4 5TF
Tel: 020 8996 3333
Fax: 020 8742 8390
www.letts-education.com

Text © Andrew Hodges, Alan Jarvis, Heather Monaghan

Series editor: Alan Jarvis
Designed, edited and produced by Gecko Limited, Cambridge
Cover design: Santamaria
Illustrations: Mike Atkinson, Lizzy Finlay, Sally Kindberg

British Library Cataloguing-in-Publication Data
A CIP record for this book is available from the British Library

ISBN 1 84085 544 4

Printed in the UK

Letts Educational Ltd, a division of Granada Learning Ltd. Part of the Granada Media Group.

Contents

How to use this book

In this book you will learn about yourself and other animals. You will also find out about how animals move, feed and grow. You will learn about plants too, what they look like and what they need for growing.

Look out for these.

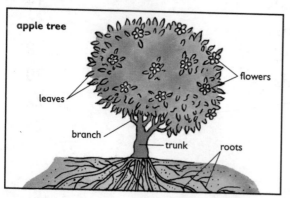

Labels on pictures name the parts.

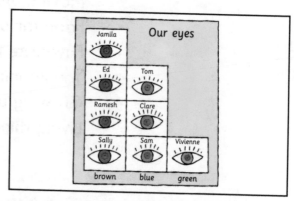

A bar chart shows how many of each kind.

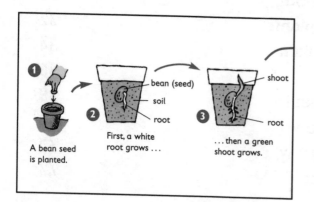

Numbers show what happens next.

Speech bubbles tell you what the children are finding out.

Ourselves

You will learn:

- about your body and some of its different parts.
- how humans are alike and how they are different.
- about your five senses.
- that humans are animals.
- about different animals and how they move.
- how people and other animals change as they get older.
- why people and other animals need food and drink.
- that animals are living things.

Growing plants

You will learn:

- about different plants and where they grow.
- how plants are alike and how they are different.
- the parts of plants.
- about plants that we eat.
- about other foods that come from plants.
- about plant roots.
- how seeds grow.
- how to find out if plants need light to grow.
- why plants need water.
- that plants are living things.

Everyone is different. No-one is just like you.

Tim and Tom look very different.

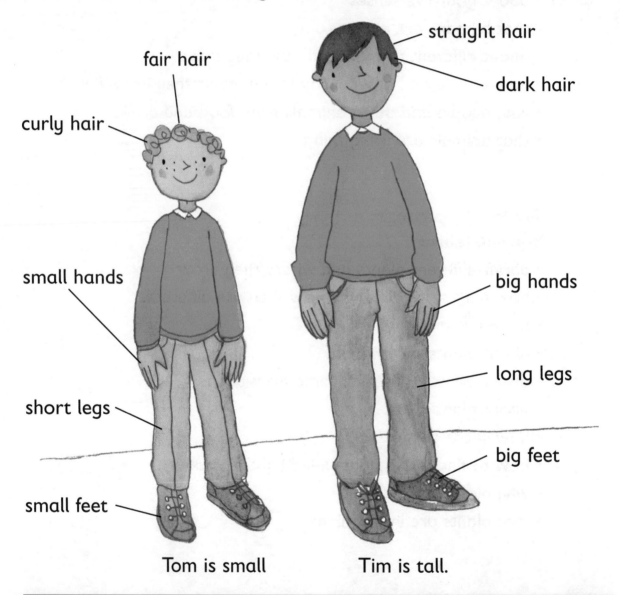

fair hair

curly hair

straight hair

dark hair

small hands

big hands

short legs

long legs

small feet

big feet

Tom is small

Tim is tall.

Draw yourself and colour your eyes and hair.
Look at your friend. How are you different?

6

Tom's group found out about the colour of their eyes.

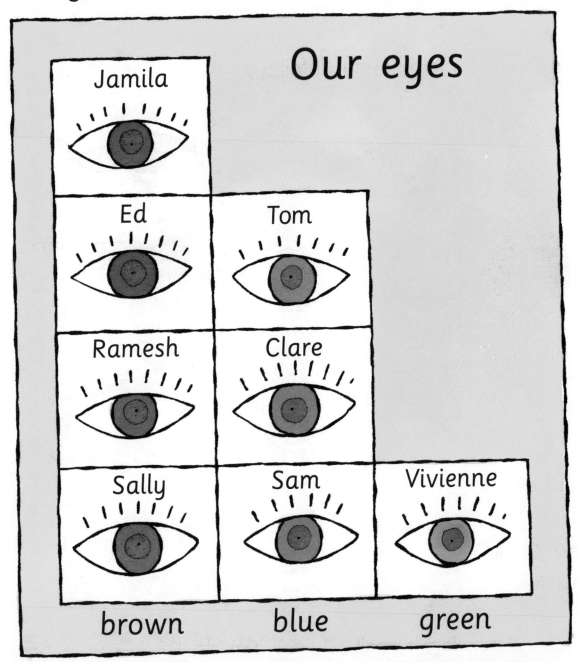

Our eyes

| brown | blue | green |

Find out about your class.
Make a chart of eye colours like this one.

Our bodies have many parts.

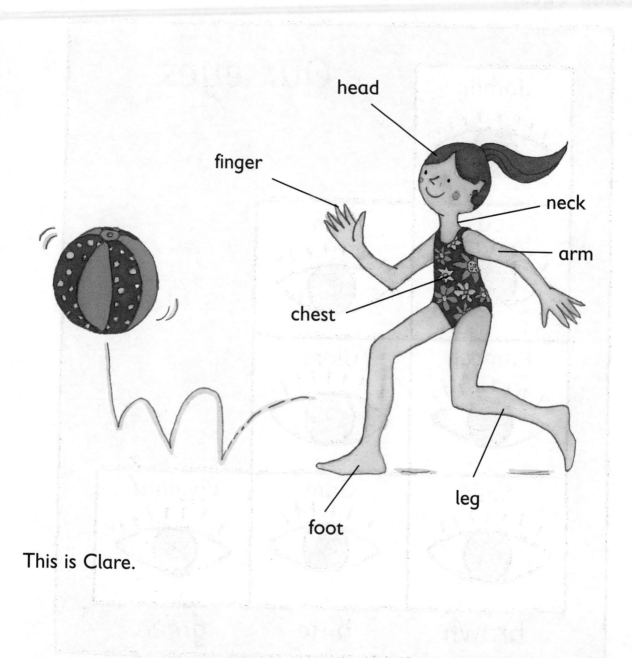

head

finger

neck

arm

chest

leg

foot

This is Clare.

Point to these parts of your body.
Play the game 'Simon says'.

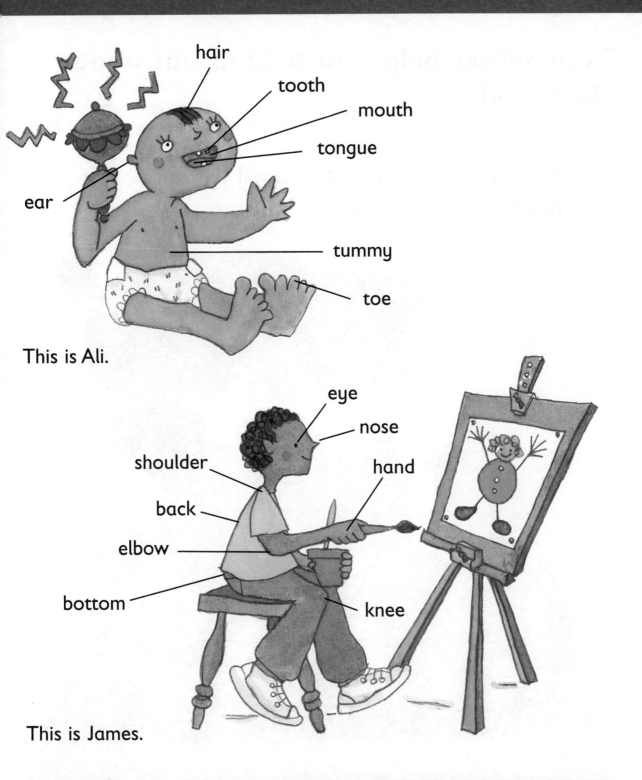

hair

tooth

mouth

tongue

ear

tummy

toe

This is Ali.

eye

nose

shoulder

hand

back

elbow

bottom

knee

This is James.

Use these pages to help you label a picture of yourself.

Your senses help you to find out about the world.

You hear with your ears. You smell with your nose. You touch with your skin.

Play a pencil and paper game. Close your eyes and try to draw a face. Try to write your name.

You see with your eyes. You taste with your tongue.

What can these children see, hear, taste, touch and smell?

senses

Humans are animals.

There are lots of different kinds of animals.

Animals can be big.

Animals can be small.

Some animals have a hard shell . . .

. . . and some have a soft body.

Talk about other animals. What are they like?

Some animals can fly . . .

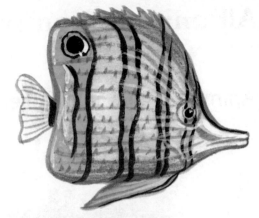

. . . and some can swim.

Some can peel bananas . . .

. . . and some can read books.

Draw some animals. Don't forget to draw yourself!

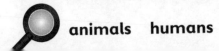 animals humans

13

All animals can move around.

Animals move in different ways.

The rabbit hops quickly.

The slug slides slowly.

The horse gallops.

The fish swims.

Play a guessing game. Move along like an animal.
Can your friend guess what animal you are?

Animals move different parts of their bodies.

The bird flaps its wings.

The spider crawls.

The cow bends its neck.

The frog jumps.

Think of some other animals. Find out how they move.

animals

All animals need food and drink.

Many animals find their own food.

Spiders can catch flies.

Cows eat grass.

Some birds eat berries.

Cats can catch mice.

Talk about the food other animals eat.

Pet animals cannot find their own food.
We must give them food and drink.

Tim and Jamila
look after a pet
hamster.

How would you look after this pet?

Talk about how to look after other pet animals.

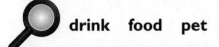

drink   food   pet

You need to eat and drink to stay alive.

Tom and his friends are hungry.
They choose their lunch.

rice

Pasta

chicken

Pizza

I've got pasta.

Chicken, please.

Pizza, please.

Draw some food that you like to eat.

After lunch, they made a chart of the food they chose.

What can you find out from the chart?
What do your friends like to drink? Make a chart.

drink   food   hungry

19

Some young animals look like their parents.

These kittens look like their parents.

The kittens get bigger and heavier as they grow up.

The kittens grow up into cats.

Find all the ways the kittens look like the mother cat and the father cat.

Do you think these animals look like their parents?

Frogs and tadpoles look very different.
Find out about them.

 parent

We change as we grow up and get older.

This is Wilf. How does he change?

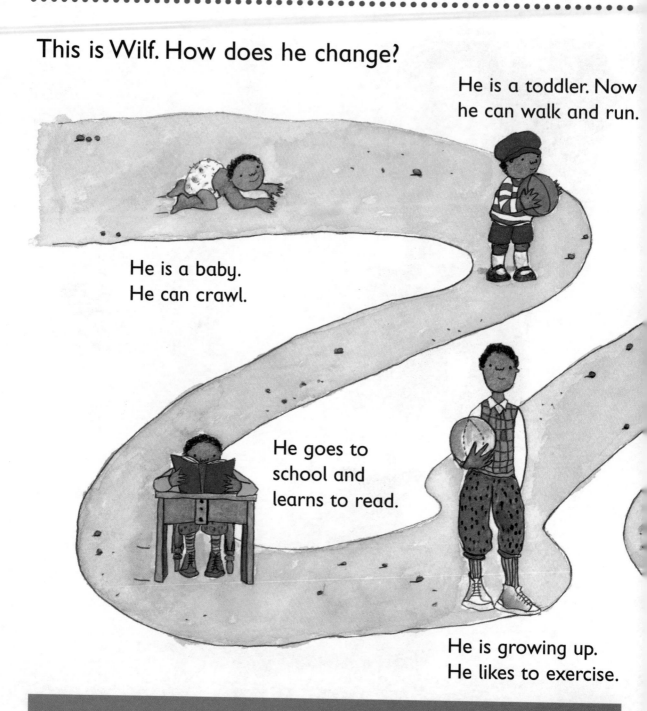

He is a toddler. Now he can walk and run.

He is a baby.
He can crawl.

He goes to school and learns to read.

He is growing up.
He likes to exercise.

Talk about how Wilf looks different as he gets older.

He is grown-up and leaves school.

He is getting older.

This is Wilf today. He is an old man.

Will you be taller next year?
Find out if the oldest people in your class are the tallest.

 baby grow toddler

Animals are living things.

All animals need food and drink. They can move around.

Which of these can eat?

Which one can drink?

Which one can move on its own?

Draw an animal that can eat and move.

All animals use their senses. Which of these can see or hear or feel or taste or smell?

Find some pictures to cut out. Sort them into two groups: 'alive' and 'not alive'.

 animals   drink   food   living things   senses

There are lots of different plants.

These are all plants, but they look very different.

Some plants are tall . . .

. . . and some are small.

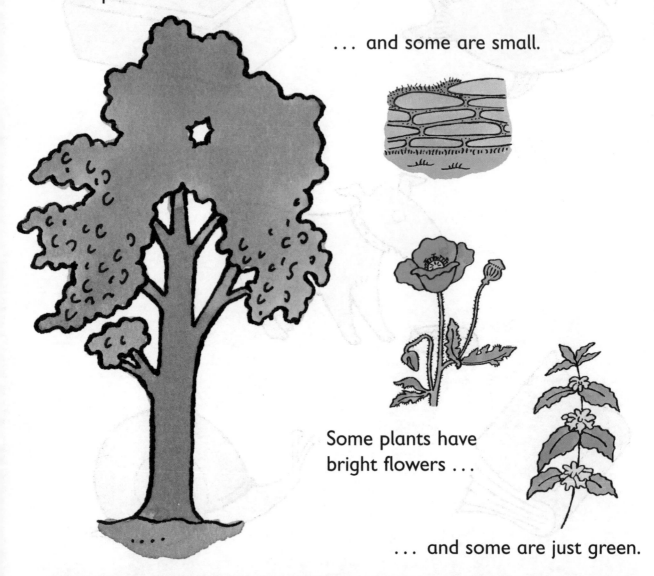

Some plants have
bright flowers . . .

. . . and some are just green.

Talk about how these plants are different from each other.

Some plants grow in fields . . .   . . . some grow in ponds.

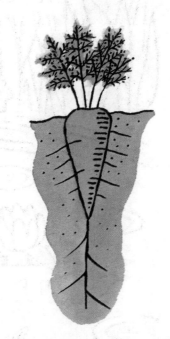

Some are called weeds . . .   . . . some are called vegetables.

Look at plants around your school, but do not pick them.
Find a plant you like and draw it. Write a sentence about it.

 grow   plants   vegetables   weeds

Plants grow in different places.

There are plants growing near your school.

moss

rushes

duckweed

pondweed

Talk about where these plants are growing.

People grow some plants, but lots of wild plants grow on their own.

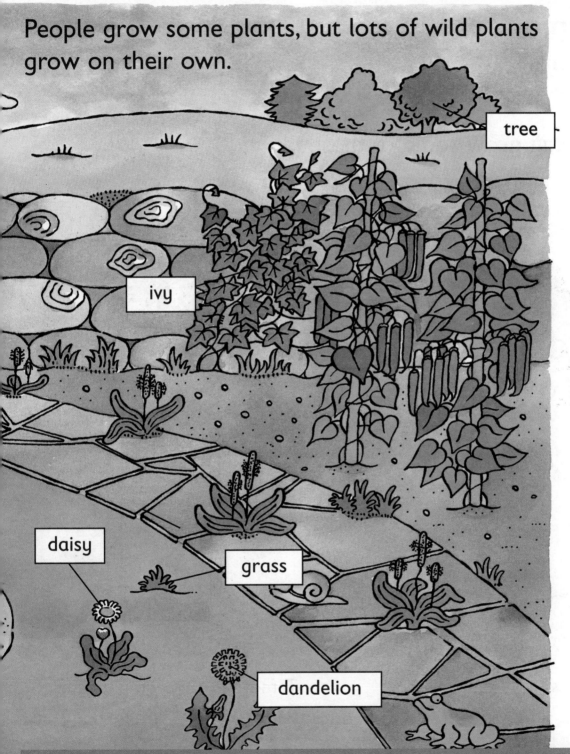

tree

ivy

daisy

grass

dandelion

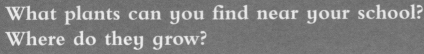

What plants can you find near your school?
Where do they grow?

Humans eat food that comes from plants.

We can grow some of these plants.

Apples grow on trees.

Tomatoes grow on plants in a greenhouse.

Find out where pears and cabbages grow.

These plants grow in a vegetable garden.

Potatoes grow under the ground.

Peas grow inside the pods of a pea plant.

Find and draw some other plants that grow in a vegetable garden.

 humans   food   grow   vegetables

Most of the foods you eat come from plants.

These are fruits.

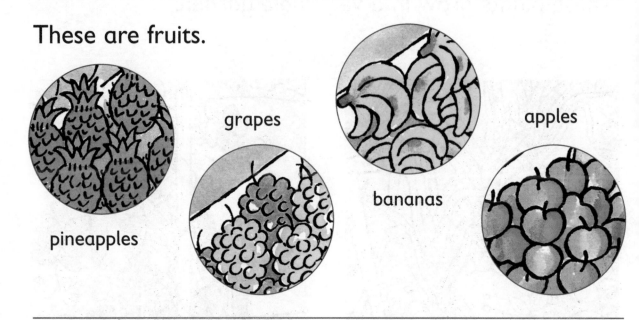

pineapples

grapes

bananas

apples

These are vegetables.

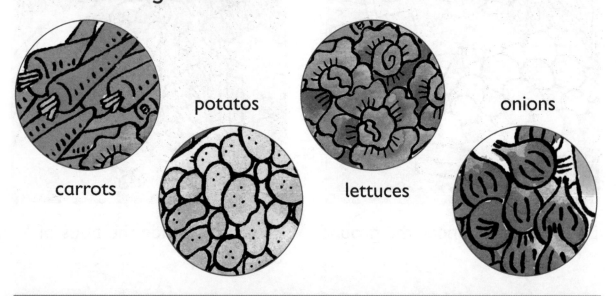

carrots

potatos

lettuces

onions

Find some more fruits and vegetables.
Put them into groups.

Most of these foods come from plants too.

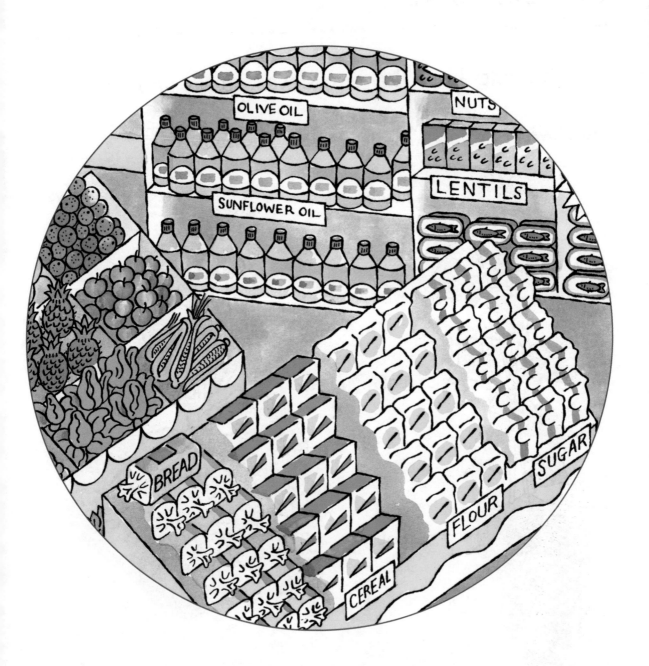

Talk about which foods come from plants that we can grow in this country.

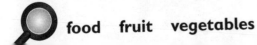
food   fruit   vegetables

Plants look very different but they have the same parts.

These plants have flowers, leaves, stems and roots.

sunflower

daisy

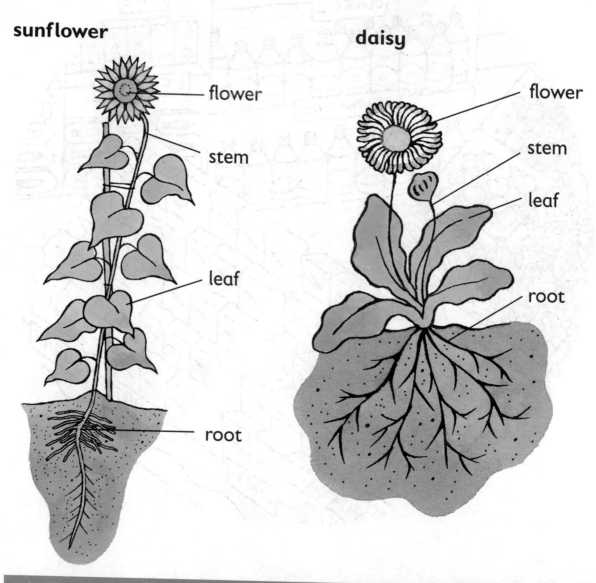

Find other plants that have these parts.
Draw and label them.

Trees have leaves, branches, trunks and roots.
Some trees have flowers in the spring.

apple tree

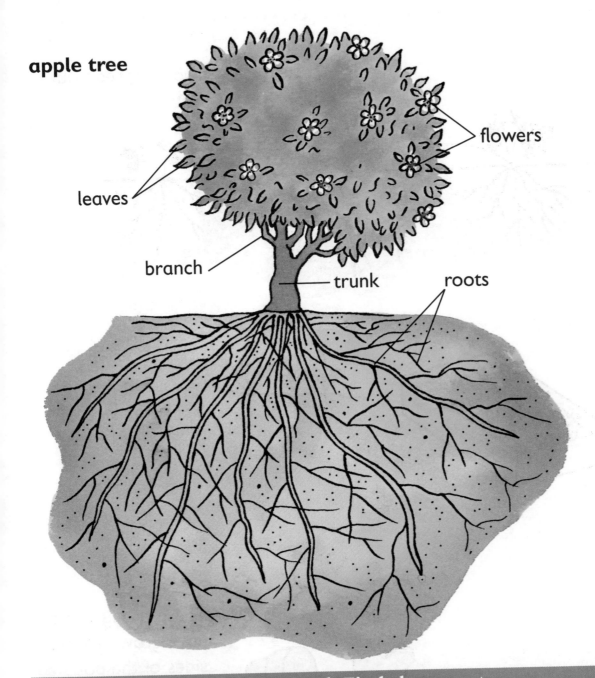

leaves

flowers

branch

trunk

roots

Look at trees near your school. Find these parts.
Make some leaf prints.

leaves   plants   roots   stem   trees

Most plants have roots that grow under the ground.

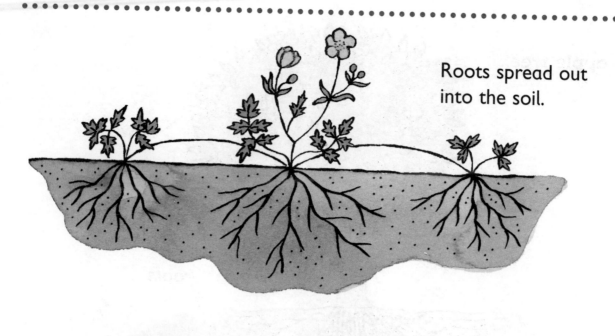

Roots spread out into the soil.

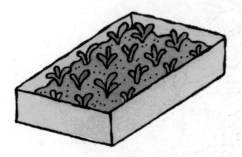

Seedlings have tiny roots.

These pansy roots have grown to the sides of the pot.

Plant roots are often thin and white.

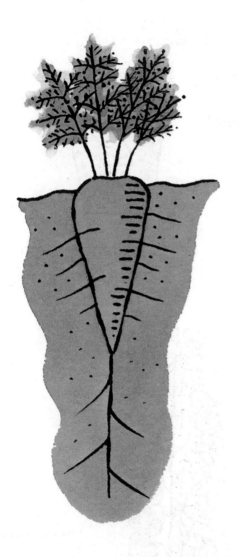

A carrot has tiny roots.

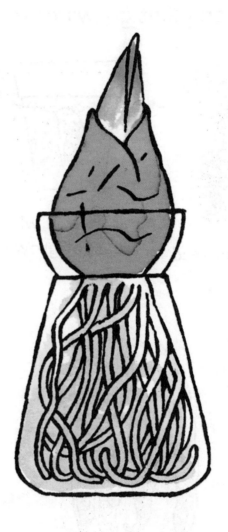

Hyacinth roots grow long in water.

Look at the plants on these pages. Find their roots. How are they different?

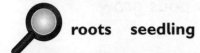

roots   seedling

Plants grow from seeds.

A bean plant grows from a bean seed.

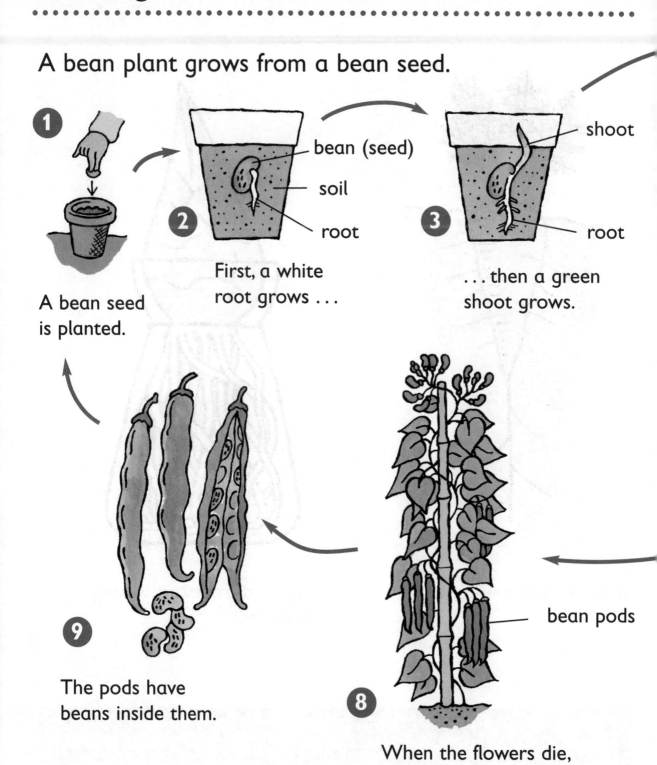

1 A bean seed is planted.

2 bean (seed)

soil

root

First, a white root grows . . .

3 shoot

root

. . . then a green shoot grows.

9 The pods have beans inside them.

8 bean pods

When the flowers die, the bean pods grow.

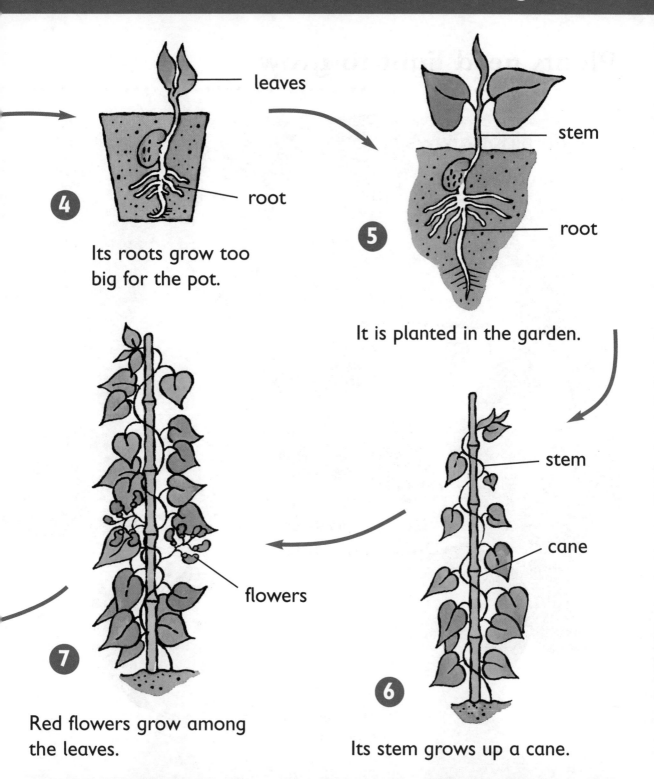

4 Its roots grow too big for the pot.

5 It is planted in the garden.

6 Its stem grows up a cane.

7 Red flowers grow among the leaves.

Plant your own bean and watch it grow.
Write about how the plant grows in a 'bean diary'.

 grow   leaves   roots   seeds   shoot   stem

Plants need light to grow.

Why does Mum put plants on the windowsill?

They get lots of light there.

Do you think plants need light to grow?
How can you find out?

Try this test. You need two plants.

Put one in a light place.

Put one in a dark place.

When will you look at the plants?

Will you water them?

What do you think will happen to the plants?

grow   light   plants   test

Plants and seeds need water to grow.

1

These seeds will not grow in the packet because there is no water.

2

When the seeds are planted, they need some water.

3

The seedlings need water to grow.

4

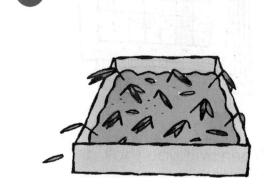

If they do not get water, they will die.

Plants need water to stay alive.

We must look after plants that are indoors.

Plants that grow outside get water when it rains.

Find out for yourself if plants and seeds need water to grow. What will you do?

 grow   seeds   water

Plants are living things. Living things can grow.

Look at the plants on this page. Some are alive and some are not alive.

These are paper flowers.

These are plastic flowers.

This plant is growing.

This plant has died.

Plants that are alive can grow.

These flowers will
live for a short time.

These wild flowers will keep on
growing. Do not pick them.

**Find pictures of wild flowers.
Draw one flower and write its name.**

 grow   living things   plants   wild flowers

45

Useful science words

animals One of the two big groups of living things. (The other one is plants.) Animals need food and drink to stay alive. They can move about, grow and use their senses.

baby A very young human or other animal.

drink Animals need to drink water. Plants do not drink.

food All animals need food to stay alive. We eat lots of different foods but most of it comes from plants.

fruit Part of a plant. We can eat some fruits, like apples, grapes and bananas.

grow When something grows it gets bigger. People grow as they get older.

humans Humans are animals. You are a human animal. All humans are the same in some ways but everyone is different.

hungry When you feel hungry, your body is telling you that you need to eat.

leaves Part of a plant. Most plant leaves are green.

light Plants need light to grow. Animals also need light to see things.

living things Animals and plants are living things.

parent An adult with young ones.

pet People keep pet animals in their homes. A pet needs food and fresh water and a clean place to live.

plants One of the two big groups of living things. (The other one is animals.) Some animals only eat plants.

roots Part of a plant. The roots help to stop the plant from falling over. Most roots grow underground in the soil.

seedling A young plant that has grown from a seed.

seeds Part of a plant. A seed can grow into a new plant. You can see the seeds on some plants, like on a sunflower. Other seeds are hidden, like bean seeds in a pod.

senses Humans have five senses. We can hear, see, touch, smell and taste things. This helps us to find out about the world around us.

shoot The small green part of a growing seed that pokes up above the ground.

stem A stem is part of a plant. The stem holds the plant up.

test A scientific way of finding out about something.

Useful science words

toddler　　A young child who is just learning to walk.

trees　　Trees are big plants. They grow from seeds. The stem of a tree is called a trunk.

vegetables　　Parts of plants that we can eat, such as carrots, peas and lettuce.

water　　Plants need water to grow. All living things need water to stay alive.

weeds　　These are plants that grow where people don't want them to, such as dandelions growing in a lawn.

wild flowers　　Some wild plants have flowers. You should not pick these wild flowers. Leave them for everyone to enjoy.

wild plants　　These are plants that grow in the countryside and on waste ground in towns. No-one plants them.